Tiktok Ad

TikTok Advertising 101: A Crash Course for Ad Beginners

Maximizing Reach, Engagement, and Conversions on TikTok: Essential Strategies for Novice Advertisers

JAMES BRANDY

TABLE OF CONTENTS

Introduction to TikTok Advertising

TikTok, the rapidly expanding social media sensation, has transformed into a formidable marketing platform, offering unparalleled opportunities for brands to engage with diverse audiences globally. In this book, we delve into the dynamic world of TikTok advertising, providing novice marketers with a comprehensive guide to navigating this vibrant landscape.

Overview of TikTok as a Marketing Platform

TikTok's explosive growth and innovative content formats have redefined the digital advertising landscape. From captivating short videos to interactive challenges, TikTok offers a myriad of creative avenues for brands to connect with users in authentic and meaningful ways. Our book explores the various features and functionalities of TikTok, offering insights into how businesses can leverage its unique platform dynamics to amplify their marketing efforts.

Importance of TikTok Ads for Beginners

For novice advertisers, TikTok presents an unparalleled opportunity to establish a presence in a rapidly evolving digital ecosystem. As traditional advertising channels face saturation, TikTok offers a breath of fresh air, enabling brands to reach elusive younger demographics and engage with them on a deeper level. Through targeted advertising campaigns, businesses can not only enhance their brand visibility but also drive tangible results, making TikTok ads an indispensable tool in today's marketing arsenal.

Creating a TikTok Ads Manager Account

To embark on your journey into TikTok advertising, the first step is to create a TikTok Ads Manager account. This account serves as your gateway to accessing powerful advertising tools and resources tailored to your marketing objectives. Follow these simple steps to kickstart your advertising endeavors:

Sign Up: Navigate to the TikTok Ads Manager platform and click on the "Sign Up" button to initiate the account creation process. Provide the required information, including your email address and password, to register your account.

Open Your Account: Once you've completed the registration process, log in to your newly created TikTok Ads Manager account. Familiarize yourself with the interface and explore the various features available to advertisers. Take note of essential functionalities such as campaign creation, audience targeting, and ad performance monitoring.

Navigating the TikTok Ads Manager Interface

Understanding the TikTok Ads Manager interface is crucial for efficiently managing your advertising campaigns and maximizing their impact. Here's a brief overview of key elements within the Ads Manager interface:

Dashboard: The main hub where you can access an overview of your active campaigns, ad spend, and performance metrics at a glance.

Campaigns Tab: Navigate to this section to create, edit, or monitor the performance of your advertising campaigns. Here, you can set campaign objectives, define targeting criteria, and allocate budgets.

Ad Groups: Within each campaign, you can organize your ads into ad groups based on specific targeting parameters or themes.

Creative Library: Store and manage your ad creatives, including images, videos, and ad copies, for easy access when setting up new campaigns or ad variations.

Reports and Insights: Access comprehensive analytics and performance reports to evaluate the effectiveness of your campaigns and identify areas for optimization.

By mastering the process of creating a TikTok Ads Manager account and navigating its interface, you'll lay a solid foundation for launching successful advertising campaigns on TikTok.

Exploring Different Ad Formats

TikTok offers a variety of ad formats tailored to suit different marketing objectives and audience preferences. Here are some of the key ad formats you can leverage:

In-Feed Ads: These ads seamlessly integrate into users' "For You" feed, appearing alongside organic content. They typically feature engaging videos that capture users' attention as they scroll through their feeds [5].

Branded Hashtag Challenges: Branded hashtag challenges encourage user participation by inviting them to create and share content around a specific hashtag theme. Brands can sponsor these challenges to increase brand awareness and engagement [3].

TopView Ads: These ads are the first thing users see when they open the TikTok app. They consist of high-impact videos or images that capture users' attention, making them ideal for delivering a strong brand message [5].

Branded Effects: Branded effects allow brands to enhance users' content creation experience by providing interactive filters, stickers, and special effects. These effects can be customized to align with the brand's identity and messaging [4].

Spark Ads: Spark ads are immersive, full-screen ads that offer a rich multimedia experience, combining images, videos, and interactive elements. They are designed to captivate users' attention and drive engagement [5].

Choosing the Right Ad Setup for Your Campaign

Selecting the most suitable ad format depends on various factors, including your campaign objectives, target audience, and budget. Consider the following when choosing an ad format:

Objective Alignment: Ensure the chosen ad format aligns with your campaign goals, whether it's increasing brand awareness, driving app installs, or boosting website traffic.

Audience Engagement: Evaluate which ad format resonates best with your target audience and encourages the desired level of engagement.

Creative Assets: Assess your available creative resources and determine which ad format allows you to effectively showcase your brand message and offerings.

Budget Considerations: Take into account the cost associated with each ad format and choose one that offers the best value for your advertising budget.

By understanding the unique characteristics of each TikTok ad format and considering your campaign objectives, audience preferences, and resources, you can make informed decisions to maximize the effectiveness of your advertising efforts.

CHAPTER THREE

Crafting Compelling Ad Creatives

Design Principles for Effective TikTok Ads

When creating TikTok ads, it's essential to adhere to design principles that resonate with the platform's audience. Here are key principles to consider:

TikTok-first Approach: Design ads that align with TikTok's vibrant and dynamic aesthetic to captivate users' attention from the moment they appear on their feed [1].

Visual Impact: Utilize vibrant colors, high-quality images, and eye-catching graphics to create visually appealing ads that stand out amidst users' feeds [6].

Concise Messaging: Keep ad content concise and to the point, conveying the message effectively within the limited duration of TikTok videos. Clear and concise messaging enhances user engagement and comprehension [4].

Tips for Creating Engaging Ad Content

Crafting compelling ad content is crucial for capturing users' attention and driving meaningful engagement. Here are some tips for creating engaging TikTok ad content:

Storytelling: Tell a compelling story that resonates with your target audience, evoking emotions and sparking curiosity. Effective storytelling enhances brand recall and fosters a deeper connection with users [4].

User-generated Content: Incorporate user-generated content into your ads to leverage the authenticity and relatability it offers. Encourage user participation and engagement by featuring content created by your audience [5].

Interactive Elements: Implement interactive elements such as polls, quizzes, and challenges to encourage user interaction and participation. Interactive ads not only capture users' attention but also foster a sense of involvement and immersion [5].

By adhering to design principles tailored to TikTok's audience and implementing engaging content strategies, advertisers can create compelling ad creatives that resonate with users and drive meaningful results.

Identifying Your Target Audience on TikTok

Understanding TikTok Demographics: Begin by analyzing TikTok's user demographics to identify your target audience. Consider factors such as age, gender, location, interests, and behavior patterns [6].

Utilizing TikTok's Ad Targeting Options: Take advantage of TikTok's robust ad targeting options, including demographic targeting, interest targeting, behavior targeting, and custom audience targeting. Tailor your ad campaigns to reach specific segments of TikTok users most likely to engage with your content [6].

Leveraging Lookalike Audiences: Use lookalike audiences to expand your reach and target users similar to your existing customer base. By leveraging data from your current audience, TikTok can identify and target users who share similar characteristics and behaviors [6].

Testing and Refining Targeting Strategies: Continuously test and refine your targeting strategies based on campaign performance metrics. Monitor key performance indicators (KPIs) such as click-through rates, conversion rates, and return on ad spend (ROAS) to optimize your targeting efforts over time [6].

Budgeting Best Practices for Ad Beginners

Starting with Open Budgets: Begin your ad campaigns with open budgets to allow TikTok's algorithm to optimize ad delivery and maximize reach. Open budgets provide flexibility and enable you to allocate more resources to high-performing campaigns [4].

Choosing Daily Budgets Over Lifetime Budgets: Opt for daily budgets rather than lifetime budgets to maintain greater control over your campaign spending. Daily budgets allow you to set a maximum daily spending limit, ensuring that your budget is distributed evenly throughout the campaign duration [4].

Monitoring Campaign Performance: Regularly monitor your campaign performance metrics to assess the effectiveness of your budget allocation. Adjust your budgets based on campaign performance data, reallocating resources to campaigns that deliver the best results [4].

Testing Different Budget Levels: Experiment with different budget levels to determine the optimal investment for your ad campaigns. Start with smaller budgets and gradually increase spending as you identify successful targeting and creative strategies [4].

By identifying your target audience on TikTok and implementing budgeting best practices, you can optimize your ad campaigns for maximum effectiveness and return on investment (ROI).

Launching your first TikTok ad campaign can be an exciting endeavor, but it requires careful planning and execution to ensure success. This chapter provides a step-by-step guide to creating your initial ad campaign on TikTok, along with common mistakes to avoid for new advertisers.

Step-by-Step Guide to Creating Your Initial Ad Campaign

Set Campaign Objectives: Define clear and measurable goals for your ad campaign, such as increasing brand awareness, driving website traffic, or boosting app installations.

Access TikTok Ads Manager: Log in to your TikTok Ads Manager account and navigate to the Campaigns tab to begin creating a new campaign.

Select Campaign Objective: Choose the appropriate campaign objective that aligns with your goals, such as Traffic, Conversions, App Installations, or Brand Awareness.

Define Target Audience: Single out your target audience based on demographics, interests, and behaviors. Utilize TikTok's targeting options to reach the most relevant users for your campaign.

Set Ad Group Details: Specify the details for your ad group, including budget, schedule, bidding strategy, and targeting options.

Create Ad Creative: Develop engaging ad creative that captures the attention of TikTok users. Consider using video content, compelling visuals, and catchy captions to convey your message effectively.

Review and Launch Campaign: Review all campaign details to ensure accuracy and alignment with your objectives. Once satisfied, launch your ad campaign to start reaching your target audience on TikTok.

Common Mistakes to Avoid for New Advertisers

Ignoring Targeting Options: Failing to utilize TikTok's advanced targeting options can result in ads being shown to irrelevant audiences, leading to wasted ad spend and poor campaign performance.

Poor Ad Creative: Neglecting to invest time and effort into creating high-quality ad creative can diminish the effectiveness of your campaign. Ensure your ads are visually pleasing, engaging, and aligned with your brand identity.

Overlooking Campaign Optimization: Neglecting to monitor and optimize your ad campaigns can prevent you from maximizing results. Regularly analyze campaign performance data and make adjustments to improve targeting, creative, and budget allocation.

Setting Unrealistic Expectations: Expecting immediate success with your first ad campaign on TikTok can lead to disappointment. Understand that success may take time and requires continuous testing and optimization.

Ignoring Feedback and Data: Disregarding feedback from users and campaign performance data can hinder your ability to improve future campaigns. Pay attention to user engagement metrics and adjust your strategies accordingly.

By following this step-by-step guide and avoiding common mistakes, you can launch your first TikTok ad campaign with confidence and set the foundation for future success.

To achieve maximum success with your TikTok ad campaigns, it's essential to continually analyze and optimize their performance. This chapter delves into the intricacies of analyzing TikTok ad metrics and implementing iterative strategies for continuous improvement.

Analyzing TikTok Ad Metrics

Impressions: Measure the number of times your ad is displayed to users. High impression counts indicate strong visibility, but it's crucial to assess other metrics for deeper insights.

Engagement Rate: Evaluate how users interact with your ad, including likes, comments, shares, and clicks. A high engagement rate signifies compelling content that resonates with the audience.

Click-Through Rate (CTR): Calculate the percentage of users who click on your ad after viewing it. A higher CTR indicates that your ad effectively captures users' attention and encourages action.

Conversion Rate: Track the percentage of users who complete a desired action, such as making a purchase or signing up for a newsletter, after clicking on your ad. A high conversion rate indicates successful ad performance in driving desired outcomes.

Return on Ad Spend (ROAS): Measure the revenue generated for every dollar spent on advertising. ROAS helps assess the effectiveness of your ad campaigns in generating profitable returns.

Cost per Acquisition (CPA): Determine the average cost incurred to acquire a new customer or lead. Optimizing CPA involves minimizing advertising costs while maximizing conversions.

Iterative Strategies for Continuous Improvement

A/B Testing: Experiment with different ad creatives, messaging, targeting options, and bidding strategies to identify the most effective combinations. Continuously test and iterate to refine your approach based on performance data.

Audience Segmentation: Divide your target audience into smaller segments based on demographics, interests, or behaviors. Tailor ad content and targeting strategies to each segment to enhance relevance and engagement.

Ad Creative Optimization: Regularly refresh and optimize your ad creative to maintain user interest and prevent ad fatigue. Experiment with new visuals, messaging, and formats to capture attention and drive engagement.

Budget Allocation: Allocate your ad budget strategically based on the performance of different campaigns, ad sets, and targeting options. Shift budget towards top-performing assets and scale successful campaigns for maximum impact.

Campaign Optimization: Monitor ad performance metrics closely and make data-driven adjustments to optimize campaign settings, targeting parameters, and bidding strategies. Continuously refine your approach to improve ROI and achieve your advertising goals.

Implementing these iterative strategies and leveraging insights from TikTok ad metrics allows you to optimize ad performance over time, drive better results, and maximize the return on your advertising investment.

CHAPTER SEVEN

Advanced Tips and Tricks

In this chapter, we explore advanced strategies for leveraging TikTok trends and harnessing collaborations and partnerships to amplify the reach and success of your ad campaigns.

Leveraging TikTok Trends for Ad Success

Stay Current: Continuously monitor TikTok trends, including challenges, memes, and viral content. Align your ad content with popular trends to tap into the platform's organic reach and engagement.

Creative Adaptation: Seamlessly integrate trending themes, sounds, and formats into your ad creative while ensuring alignment with your brand identity and messaging. Leverage popular hashtags and cultural references to resonate with TikTok's diverse user base.

User-Generated Content (UGC): Encourage user participation by incorporating UGC elements into your ads, such as featuring customer testimonials, reviews, or user-generated videos. Leverage the authenticity and relatability of UGC to establish trust and credibility with your audience.

Embrace Creativity: Think outside the box and experiment with unconventional ideas and storytelling techniques. Embrace TikTok's creative culture and embrace bold, innovative approaches to captivate users' attention and spark engagement.

Collaborations and Partnerships for Amplified Reach

Identify Influencers: Collaborate with popular TikTok influencers whose content aligns with your brand values and target audience. Leverage influencers' existing fan base and credibility to extend the reach and impact of your ad campaigns.

Co-Creation: Work closely with influencers to co-create engaging ad content that seamlessly integrates your brand message with their authentic style and voice. Foster genuine partnerships that prioritize authenticity and resonate with their followers.

Sponsored Content: Partner with influencers to develop sponsored content that highlights your brand naturally and compellingly. Provide influencers with creative freedom while ensuring alignment with your campaign objectives and messaging.

Cross-Promotion: Explore opportunities for cross-promotion with complementary brands or TikTok accounts to reach new audiences and enhance brand visibility. Collaborate on joint campaigns or content initiatives to leverage each other's followers and engagement.

Track Performance: Monitor the performance of collaborations and partnerships using relevant metrics, such as engagement, reach, and conversion rates. Evaluate the effectiveness of each partnership and adjust your approach based on performance insights.

By leveraging TikTok trends and cultivating strategic collaborations and partnerships, you can unlock new opportunities for ad success, amplify your reach, and establish a strong presence on the platform.

CHAPTER EIGHT

Case Studies and Success Stories

In this chapter, we delve into real-world examples of successful TikTok ad campaigns, providing valuable insights and learnings that advertisers can apply to their strategies.

Examining Successful TikTok Ad Campaigns

Chipotle: #GuacDance Challenge

Chipotle launched a campaign encouraging users to show off their dance moves for free guacamole. The challenge went viral, garnering millions of user-generated videos and significantly boosting brand engagement and awareness.

Fenty Beauty: #FentyBeautyHouse

Fenty Beauty partnered with TikTok influencers to create content showcasing their products. By leveraging influencer partnerships and user-generated content, Fenty Beauty successfully engaged with their target audience and drove sales.

Elf Cosmetics: #EyesLipsFace

Elf Cosmetics launched a catchy and memorable campaign featuring their #EyesLipsFace song. The campaign generated over 6 billion views and increased brand awareness among TikTok's younger demographic.

The Washington Post: #ReadTheFacts

The Washington Post utilized TikTok to combat misinformation by launching the #ReadTheFacts campaign. Through engaging and informative content, they effectively promoted the importance of credible journalism and fact-checking.

Learning from Real-world Examples

Authenticity: Authenticity is key to resonating with TikTok's audience. Successful campaigns often embrace TikTok's creative culture and foster genuine connections with users.

Creativity: Creativity plays a crucial role in capturing users' attention on TikTok. Brands should prioritize innovative and entertaining content that stands out amidst the platform's diverse content landscape.

Engagement: Engagement is a fundamental metric for measuring the success of TikTok ad campaigns. By encouraging user participation and fostering community interaction, brands can drive meaningful engagement and build brand loyalty.

Adaptability: TikTok is a dynamic platform with rapidly evolving trends and user behaviors. Successful brands stay adaptable and responsive, continuously iterating their strategies based on performance data and emerging trends.

Collaboration: Collaborating with influencers and leveraging user-generated content can significantly amplify the reach and impact of TikTok ad campaigns. Brands should identify relevant partners and foster collaborative relationships to enhance campaign effectiveness.

By examining successful TikTok ad campaigns and drawing insights from real-world examples, advertisers can gain valuable knowledge and inspiration to optimize their strategies and drive results on the platform.

CHAPTER NINE

Future Trends in TikTok Advertising

In this chapter, we explore the evolving landscape of TikTok advertising and strategies for anticipating and adapting to emerging trends to stay ahead of the curve.

Anticipating and Adapting to Emerging Trends

Short-Form Video Evolution: As short-form video continues to dominate social media, TikTok is expected to evolve its format and features to keep users engaged. Advertisers should anticipate shifts in video consumption habits and adapt their content to align with emerging trends.

Interactive and Immersive Experiences: Future trends may see an increased focus on interactive and immersive ad experiences. Brands can leverage features like augmented reality (AR) filters, gamification, and interactive storytelling to create engaging content that resonates with TikTok's audience.

Personalized and Data-Driven Targeting: With advancements in data analytics and machine learning, advertisers can expect more sophisticated targeting capabilities on TikTok. Personalized ads tailored to users' interests, behaviors, and demographics can enhance relevance and drive better campaign performance.

E-commerce Integration: TikTok's growing influence as a shopping destination presents opportunities for e-commerce integration within the platform. Brands can anticipate the integration of seamless shopping experiences, including shoppable ads, product catalogs, and in-app purchases, to facilitate direct conversions.

Brand Safety and Transparency: As advertisers prioritize brand safety and transparency, TikTok is likely to implement stricter policies and tools to ensure ad integrity. Advertisers should stay informed about platform updates and proactively address any concerns regarding ad placement and content authenticity.

Staying Ahead in the Evolving Landscape

Continuous Learning and Experimentation: Advertisers should adopt a mindset of continuous learning and experimentation to stay ahead of evolving trends. By staying curious, testing new strategies, and analyzing results, brands can identify emerging opportunities and refine their approach accordingly.

Agility and Adaptability: The pace of change in digital advertising requires brands to be agile and adaptable. Advertisers should be prepared to pivot quickly in response to shifts in consumer behavior, platform updates, and industry trends.

Collaboration and Networking: Building relationships with industry peers, thought leaders, and platform representatives can provide valuable insights and opportunities for collaboration. Participating in industry events, forums, and networking groups can help advertisers stay informed and connected within the TikTok advertising community.

Investment in Creative Talent and Technology: As TikTok evolves, investing in creative talent and technology becomes increasingly important. Brands should prioritize hiring skilled content creators, designers, and technologists to produce high-quality and innovative ad content that resonates with TikTok's audience.

By anticipating and adapting to emerging trends in TikTok advertising, advertisers can position themselves for success in the dynamic and ever-evolving landscape of social media marketing.

CHAPTER TEN

Maximizing ROI with Performance Marketing Tactics

In this chapter, we'll delve into the realm of performance marketing tactics tailored specifically for TikTok advertising. Performance marketing focuses on driving measurable results and optimizing return on investment (ROI) through targeted strategies. Leveraging the unique features of TikTok, we'll explore how to maximize ROI and achieve your advertising objectives effectively.

Understanding Performance Marketing on TikTok

Performance marketing on TikTok revolves around precise targeting, compelling creatives, and continuous optimization to achieve specific goals, whether it's driving website traffic, increasing app installs, or boosting sales.

Harnessing TikTok's Ad Formats for Results

We'll discuss how to select the most suitable ad formats for your campaign objectives, including in-feed ads, branded hashtag challenges, and branded effects. Each format offers distinct advantages for driving performance and engaging audiences.

Implementing Advanced Targeting Strategies

Learn how to refine your audience targeting using TikTok's robust targeting options, including demographic targeting, interest targeting, and custom audiences. We'll explore best practices for reaching your ideal audience effectively.

Optimizing Ad Creative for Conversions

Discover techniques for creating compelling ad creatives that capture attention, evoke emotions, and drive action. We'll cover strategies for crafting captivating videos, compelling copy, and eye-catching visuals to maximize engagement and conversions.

Testing and Iterating for Continuous Improvement

Continuous testing and iteration are key components of performance marketing. We'll discuss how to set up A/B tests, analyze performance metrics, and iterate on your campaigns to optimize results over time.

Monitoring and Analyzing Campaign Performance

Learn how to monitor key performance indicators (KPIs) and analyze campaign data to measure success and identify areas for improvement. We'll explore essential metrics such as click-through rate (CTR), conversion rate, and return on ad spend (ROAS).

Implementing Cost Optimization Strategies

Explore tactics for optimizing your ad spend and maximizing ROI, including bid optimization, budget pacing, and ad scheduling. We'll cover strategies for minimizing wasted spend and maximizing the efficiency of your advertising budget.

Case Studies: Real-World Examples of Successful Performance Marketing Campaigns

Gain insights from real-world case studies showcasing successful TikTok performance marketing campaigns. Learn from industry leaders and discover actionable strategies you can apply to your own campaigns.

In this chapter, we'll equip you with the knowledge and strategies you need to maximize ROI and drive tangible results with performance marketing on TikTok. By implementing these tactics, you'll be able to optimize your campaigns for success and achieve your advertising goals effectively.

User-generated content (UGC) has become a powerful tool for brands seeking to amplify their presence and engagement on TikTok. In this chapter, we'll explore how to effectively harness UGC to create viral campaigns that resonate with audiences and drive organic reach.

Understanding the Power of User-Generated Content

UGC refers to any content generated by users rather than brands. It holds significant sway on TikTok due to its authenticity, relatability, and ability to foster community engagement. By tapping into UGC, brands can leverage the creativity and enthusiasm of their audience to fuel viral campaigns.

Encouraging User Participation

Learn strategies for encouraging user participation and generating UGC for your TikTok campaigns. This includes creating branded challenges, launching hashtag campaigns, and incentivizing user contributions with contests or rewards. We'll explore how to inspire your audience to become active participants in your brand's story.

Curating and Amplifying UGC

Discover how to curate and amplify UGC to maximize its impact and reach. We'll discuss best practices for identifying high-quality user content, securing permission for its use, and repurposing it across your marketing channels. Learn how to showcase user contributions authentically while aligning them with your brand's messaging and values.

Leveraging UGC for Social Proof and Trust

UGC serves as powerful social proof, signaling to potential customers that your brand is trustworthy and valued by its community. Explore strategies for leveraging UGC to build trust and credibility, from featuring customer testimonials and reviews to showcasing real-life product experiences shared by users.

Nurturing Community Engagement

UGC fosters a sense of community and belonging among your audience, driving deeper engagement and loyalty. Learn how to nurture community engagement through UGC-driven campaigns that encourage interaction, conversation, and collaboration. We'll discuss tactics for fostering meaningful connections with your audience and cultivating brand advocates.

Measuring the Impact of UGC Campaigns

Understand how to measure the impact of your UGC campaigns and track key performance metrics. From engagement rates and reach to brand sentiment and conversion rates, we'll explore the various metrics you can use to assess the success of your UGC initiatives and optimize future campaigns.

Case Studies: Successful UGC Campaigns on TikTok

Gain inspiration from real-world examples of brands that have effectively harnessed UGC to drive viral campaigns on TikTok. We'll showcase innovative UGC-driven campaigns and highlight the strategies behind their success, providing valuable insights for your own UGC initiatives.

By harnessing the power of user-generated content, brands can create authentic, engaging, and impactful campaigns that resonate with audiences and drive viral reach on TikTok. In this chapter, you'll learn how to leverage UGC to foster community engagement, build trust, and amplify your brand's presence on the platform.

Influencer marketing has emerged as a key strategy for brands looking to expand their reach and engage with target audiences on TikTok. In this chapter, we'll delve into the intricacies of navigating influencer partnerships to amplify your brand's presence on the platform.

Understanding the Role of Influencers on TikTok

Explore the role of influencers within the TikTok ecosystem and how they can help brands connect with their target demographics. We'll discuss the different types of influencers, from micro-influencers to macro-influencers, and how each can impact your brand's reach and engagement.

Identifying the Right Influencer Partners

Learn how to identify the right influencer partners for your brand by considering factors such as audience demographics, engagement rates, and brand alignment. We'll discuss strategies for conducting influencer research, vetting potential partners, and building authentic relationships that resonate with both influencers and their followers.

Crafting Effective Influencer Campaigns

Discover best practices for crafting effective influencer campaigns that align with your brand's objectives and resonate with TikTok audiences. From setting campaign goals and defining key messaging to outlining deliverables and establishing campaign timelines, we'll explore the essential elements of successful influencer collaborations.

Negotiating Partnerships and Compensation

Navigate the process of negotiating influencer partnerships and compensation agreements to ensure mutually beneficial collaborations. Learn how to approach influencers with professionalism and transparency, outline expectations clearly, and negotiate compensation packages that reflect the value of their contributions.

Maximizing Impact Through Creative Collaboration

Explore strategies for maximizing the impact of influencer partnerships through creative collaboration and co-creation. We'll discuss ways to empower influencers to showcase your brand authentically, leverage their creativity and expertise, and engage their audience in meaningful ways.

Measuring the Success of Influencer Campaigns

Understand how to measure the success of your influencer campaigns and evaluate their impact on key performance metrics. From tracking reach and engagement to monitoring brand sentiment and conversion rates, we'll discuss the tools and techniques for assessing the effectiveness of influencer partnerships.

Case Studies: Successful Influencer Collaborations on TikTok

Gain insights from real-world examples of brands that have leveraged influencer partnerships to amplify their reach and engagement on TikTok. We'll showcase innovative influencer campaigns and highlight the strategies behind their success, providing valuable lessons for your influencer marketing initiatives.

By navigating influencer partnerships strategically, brands can tap into the power of influencers to amplify their reach, engage with target audiences, and drive meaningful results on TikTok. In this chapter, you'll learn how to identify the right influencers, craft effective campaigns, negotiate partnerships, and measure success, ultimately leveraging influencer marketing to achieve your brand's objectives.

In today's digital landscape, data analytics plays a pivotal role in informing marketing strategies and driving business growth. In this chapter, we'll explore how harnessing the power of data analytics and insights can empower advertisers to make informed decisions, optimize campaign performance, and achieve their marketing objectives on TikTok.

The Importance of Data Analytics in TikTok Advertising

Understand why data analytics is crucial for TikTok's advertising success and how it enables advertisers to gain valuable insights into audience behavior, campaign performance, and market trends. We'll discuss the role of data in driving strategic decision-making and maximizing return on investment (ROI) for advertising campaigns.

Leveraging TikTok's Analytics Tools

Explore the analytics tools available on the TikTok platform and how advertisers can leverage them to track and measure various aspects of their ad campaigns. From audience demographics and engagement metrics to ad performance and conversion tracking, we'll delve into the capabilities of TikTok's analytics dashboard and how advertisers can use it to optimize their campaigns.

Key Metrics and KPIs for TikTok Advertising

Identify the key metrics and key performance indicators (KPIs) that advertisers should track to evaluate the effectiveness of their TikTok ad campaigns. We'll discuss metrics such as impressions, click-through rate (CTR), conversion rate, return on ad spend (ROAS), and more, and how they provide insights into campaign performance and audience behavior.

Data-Driven Optimization Strategies

Learn how to use data-driven optimization strategies to continuously improve the performance of your TikTok ad campaigns. We'll discuss techniques such as A/B testing, audience segmentation, ad creative optimization, and bid management, and how they can help advertisers refine their targeting, messaging, and creative assets for maximum impact.

Harnessing AI and Machine Learning for Insights

Discover how advancements in artificial intelligence (AI) and machine learning are revolutionizing data analytics in TikTok advertising. We'll explore how AI-powered algorithms can analyze vast amounts of data in real time, identify patterns and trends, and provide actionable insights that drive more effective advertising strategies.

Integrating Data Analytics Across the Marketing Funnel

Understand the importance of integrating data analytics across the marketing funnel, from awareness and consideration to conversion and retention. We'll discuss how advertisers can use data insights to personalize the customer journey, optimize ad spend allocation, and drive meaningful engagement at every stage of the funnel.

Case Studies: Data-Driven Success Stories

Explore real-world case studies of brands that have leveraged data analytics to achieve success in TikTok advertising. We'll showcase examples of how data-driven insights have informed strategic decision-making, optimized campaign performance, and delivered measurable results, providing valuable lessons for advertisers looking to unlock the power of data analytics on TikTok.

By unlocking the power of data analytics and insights, advertisers can gain a deeper understanding of their target audience, optimize their ad campaigns for maximum impact, and drive meaningful business results on TikTok. In this chapter, you'll learn how to leverage TikTok's analytics tools, track key metrics and KPIs, optimize campaigns using data-driven strategies, and harness the latest advancements in AI and machine learning to achieve advertising success.

CHAPTER FOURTEEN

Scaling Up Your Advertising Efforts for Growth

As advertisers gain confidence and success with their TikTok ad campaigns, the natural next step is to scale up their advertising efforts to achieve even greater growth and impact. In this chapter, we'll explore strategies for scaling up your advertising efforts on TikTok, from expanding your audience reach to increasing ad spend and optimizing campaign performance for sustained growth.

Assessing Readiness for Scaling Up

Before diving into scaling up your advertising efforts, it's essential to assess your readiness for growth. We'll discuss key factors to consider, such as campaign performance, budget allocation, resource availability, and organizational capacity, to determine whether your business is prepared to scale up its TikTok advertising efforts effectively.

Expanding Audience Reach and Targeting

One of the primary strategies for scaling up advertising efforts on TikTok is to expand audience reach and targeting. We'll explore advanced targeting options, including lookalike audiences, interest targeting, and custom audience segmentation, to reach new and highly relevant audiences and maximize the impact of your ad campaigns.

Increasing Ad Spend and Budget Optimization

Scaling up advertising efforts often involves increasing ad spend and budget allocation to support larger and more ambitious campaigns. We'll discuss best practices for budget optimization, including scaling budgets incrementally, monitoring performance closely, and reallocating budget to top-performing campaigns and audience segments to maximize ROI and minimize wasted ad spend.

Diversifying Ad Formats and Creative Assets

To scale up advertising efforts effectively, it's essential to diversify ad formats and creative assets to keep campaigns fresh, engaging, and relevant to your target audience. We'll explore different ad formats, creative strategies, and content types, including video ads, carousel ads, user-generated content, and influencer collaborations, to capture audience attention and drive conversion at scale.

Leveraging Automation and Technology Solutions

As advertising efforts scale up, manual campaign management becomes increasingly challenging and time-consuming. We'll discuss the role of automation and technology solutions, such as ad management platforms, AI-powered optimization tools, and programmatic advertising, in streamlining campaign management, improving efficiency, and maximizing the effectiveness of your TikTok ad campaigns.

Implementing Multi-Channel Marketing Strategies

To achieve sustained growth and maximize reach, it's essential to integrate TikTok advertising into a broader multi-channel marketing strategy. We'll explore how to leverage synergies between TikTok and other marketing channels, such as social media, search advertising, email marketing, and content marketing, to create cohesive and integrated campaigns that amplify your message and drive results across multiple touchpoints.

Scaling Up for Long-Term Success

Scaling up advertising efforts is not just about achieving short-term growth but also laying the foundation for long-term success and sustainability. We'll discuss strategies for scaling up responsibly, maintaining agility and flexibility, and adapting to changing market dynamics to ensure that your advertising efforts continue to deliver value and drive growth over the long term.

Case Studies: Successful Scaling Strategies

Throughout this chapter, we'll showcase real-world case studies of brands that have successfully scaled up their advertising efforts on TikTok. We'll explore their scaling strategies, challenges encountered, and lessons learned, providing valuable insights and inspiration for advertisers looking to take their TikTok advertising to the next level.

By implementing the strategies outlined in this chapter, advertisers can scale up their advertising efforts effectively, reach new audiences, drive meaningful growth, and achieve long-term success on TikTok. Whether you're a small business looking to expand your reach or an established brand aiming for exponential growth, this chapter will provide actionable insights and practical guidance for scaling up your TikTok advertising efforts for sustained success.

CHAPTER FIFTEEN

Staying Ahead of the Curve: Future-proofing Your Strategy

In the rapidly evolving landscape of TikTok advertising, staying ahead of the curve is essential to maintain a competitive edge and ensure long-term success. This chapter explores strategies for future-proofing your TikTok advertising strategy, anticipating emerging trends, and adapting to the evolving digital marketing landscape.

Embracing Innovation and Experimentation

To stay ahead of the curve, it's crucial to embrace innovation and experimentation in your TikTok advertising strategy. We'll discuss the importance of staying curious, testing new ad formats, creative approaches, and targeting strategies, and leveraging emerging technologies, such as augmented reality (AR), virtual reality (VR), and interactive experiences, to engage audiences in new and exciting ways.

Keeping Abreast of Platform Updates and Features

TikTok is continually evolving, with new features, tools, and updates being rolled out regularly. To future-proof your TikTok advertising strategy, it's essential to stay informed about platform updates and features and leverage them to your advantage. We'll explore how to stay abreast of platform changes, adapt your strategy accordingly, and capitalize on new opportunities to reach and engage your target audience effectively.

Harnessing the Power of Data and Analytics

Data-driven decision-making is key to future-proofing your TikTok advertising strategy. We'll delve into the importance of harnessing the power of data and analytics to gain insights into audience behavior, campaign performance, and market trends. By leveraging data and analytics tools, such as TikTok Ads Manager, Google Analytics, and third-party tracking platforms, advertisers can optimize their campaigns, identify emerging trends, and make informed strategic decisions to stay ahead of the curve.

Cultivating Agility and Adaptability

In a fast-paced and ever-changing digital landscape, agility and adaptability are essential traits for future-proofing your TikTok advertising strategy. We'll discuss strategies for cultivating agility within your organization, fostering a culture of experimentation and innovation, and empowering teams to adapt quickly to changing market dynamics, consumer preferences, and technological advancements.

Investing in Continuous Learning and Development

To stay ahead of the curve, it's crucial to invest in continuous learning and development for yourself and your team. We'll explore resources and opportunities for professional development, including industry conferences, webinars, online courses, and certification programs, to keep your skills sharp, stay updated on industry trends, and acquire new knowledge and expertise in TikTok advertising and digital marketing.

Building Strategic Partnerships and Collaborations

Collaboration is key to future-proofing your TikTok advertising strategy. We'll discuss the importance of building strategic partnerships and collaborations with industry experts, influencers, content creators, and other brands to amplify your reach, leverage complementary strengths, and stay ahead of the curve. By forging strategic alliances and fostering meaningful relationships within the TikTok ecosystem, advertisers can tap into new audiences, drive engagement, and stay ahead of emerging trends.

Conclusion

Mastering TikTok Advertising for Success

In conclusion, "TikTok Advertising 101: A Crash Course for Ad Beginners" serves as a comprehensive guide for mastering TikTok advertising and achieving success in the dynamic world of digital marketing. Throughout this book, we've explored essential concepts, strategies, and tactics to help beginners navigate the intricacies of TikTok advertising and maximize their advertising efforts.

From understanding the basics of TikTok advertising to creating compelling ad creatives, targeting the right audience, and optimizing ad performance, this book has provided readers with the knowledge and skills needed to launch successful TikTok ad campaigns. By following the step-by-step guidance outlined in this book, advertisers can effectively leverage TikTok's platform to reach their target audience, drive engagement, and achieve their advertising goals.

Moreover, we've emphasized the importance of staying informed about emerging trends, embracing innovation, and adapting to changes in the digital landscape. By staying ahead of the curve and continuously learning and evolving their strategies, advertisers can future-proof their TikTok advertising efforts and maintain a competitive edge in the ever-changing world of digital marketing.

As readers embark on their TikTok advertising journey, we encourage them to experiment, learn from their experiences, and leverage the power of data and analytics to refine their strategies and drive better results. By applying the knowledge and insights gained from this book, advertisers can unlock the full potential of TikTok advertising and propel their brands to new heights of success in the digital age.

In summary, "TikTok Advertising 101: A Crash Course for Ad Beginners" equips readers with the tools, techniques, and strategies needed to thrive in the world of TikTok advertising. Whether you're a novice advertiser looking to get started or a seasoned marketer seeking to enhance your skills, this book provides the guidance and resources you need to succeed in the exciting and ever-evolving realm of TikTok advertising.

www.ingramcontent.com/pod-product-compliance
Lightning Source LLC
Chambersburg PA
CBHW072259310526
45795CB00012B/1852